Your First 18 Years

Full-Childhood Memory Book

© 2022 JRG Craft

Made with Love for

CONTENTS

Note for the Writer 1

Year 1 (0 Years Old) 3

Year 2 (1 Year Old) 13

Year 3 (2 Years Old) 21

Year 4 (3 Years Old) 29

Year 5 (4 Years Old) 37

Year 6 (5 Years Old) 45

Year 7 (6 Years Old) 53

Year 8 (7 Years Old) 61

Year 9 (8 Years Old) 69

Year 10 (9 Years Old) 77

Year 11 (10 Years Old) 85

Year 12 (11 Years Old) 93

Year 13 (12 Years Old) 101

Year 14 (13 Years Old) 109

Year 15 (14 Years Old) 117

Year 16 (15 Years Old) 125

Year 17 (16 Years Old) 133

Year 18 (17 Years Old) 141

NOTE FOR THE WRITER

In the years ahead there will be countless special moments and precious details you will yearn to remember forever. When your child gets older, they will also crave to know about their life growing up, what they were like, and how they changed over the years. What fun places did they visit? What were their favorite activities, TV shows and foods? Who were their best friends? What did they accomplish? Their children and even grandchildren will take delight in learning these specifics as well.

As much as you will want to recall everything, though, the reality is that we forget so many cherished particulars. So much happens over 18 years, our brains cannot possibly hold onto more than a small fraction of it. But luckily you bought this book! Decades from now you will be so grateful you did! Just take an hour or so each year to document the essential information from that year, and ultimately you will have a treasure trove of remembrances preserved forever! You will be able to celebrate the good times, achievements, and personality traits; laugh about funny anecdotes and idiosyncrasies; and acknowledge the difficult times, And, you will be able to share it all with family and friends!

Enjoy!

Memorabilia

YEAR 1 (0 YEARS OLD)

Birth Details

Full Name	Isla Olivia Robertson
Date and Time of Birth	17/4/17
Place of Birth	Sheffield Hallamshire
Height	
Weight	7.25
Hair Color	Light / fair / dark.
Eye Color	blue

Reason for Your Name

We both liked it and thought it
was special, just like you.

Notes About Your Birth

Memorabilia

Your Favorite Things From This Year

Foods	
Toys	
Cuddle Buddies & Stuffed Animals	
Songs	
Shows	
Games	
Books	
Playmates	

Things We Did This Year

_____

_____

_____

_____

_____

_____

_____

_____

_____

_____

_____

Memorabilia

Your Most Notable Developments

_____

_____

_____

_____

_____

_____

Things You Loved to Do

_____

_____

_____

_____

_____

What You Were Like

_____

_____

_____

_____

_____

Memorabilia

What Your Typical Day Was Like

_____

_____

_____

_____

_____

_____

Special People in Your Life

_____

_____

_____

_____

_____

Challenges

_____

_____

_____

_____

_____

Memorabilia

Stories and Other Tidbits

Memorabilia

YEAR 2 (1 YEAR OLD)

Your Favorite Things From This Year

Foods	
Toys	
Cuddle Buddies & Stuffed Animals	
Songs	
Shows	
Games	
Books	
Playmates	

Things We Did This Year

_____

_____

_____

_____

_____

_____

_____

_____

_____

Memorabilia

Your Most Notable Developments

_____

_____

_____

_____

_____

_____

Things You Loved to Do

_____

_____

_____

_____

_____

What You Were Like

_____

_____

_____

_____

_____

Memorabilia

What Your Typical Day Was Like

_____

_____

_____

_____

_____

_____

Special People in Your Life

_____

_____

_____

_____

_____

Big Events

_____

_____

_____

_____

Memorabilia

Challenges

_____

_____

_____

_____

Stories and Other Tidbits

_____

_____

_____

_____

_____

_____

_____

_____

_____

_____

_____

_____

_____

_____

Memorabilia

Year 3 (2 Years Old)

Your Favorite Things From This Year

Foods	
Toys	
Cuddle Buddies & Stuffed Animals	
Songs	
Shows	
Games	
Books	
Playmates	

Things We Did This Year

_____

_____

_____

_____

_____

_____

_____

_____

_____

_____

Memorabilia

Your Most Notable Developments

_____

_____

_____

_____

_____

_____

Things You Loved to Do

_____

_____

_____

_____

_____

What You Were Like

_____

_____

_____

_____

_____

Memorabilia

What Your Typical Day Was Like

_____

_____

_____

_____

_____

_____

Special People in Your Life

_____

_____

_____

_____

_____

Big Events

_____

_____

_____

_____

_____

Memorabilia

Challenges

_____

_____

_____

_____

Stories and Other Tidbits

_____

_____

_____

_____

_____

_____

_____

_____

_____

_____

_____

_____

_____

_____

_____

Memorabilia

Year 4 (3 Years Old)

Your Favorite Things From This Year

Foods	
Toys	
Cuddle Buddies & Stuffed Animals	
Songs	
Shows	
Games	
Books	
Playmates	

Things We Did This Year

_____

_____

_____

_____

_____

_____

_____

_____

_____

Memorabilia

Your Most Notable Developments

_____

_____

_____

_____

_____

_____

Things You Loved to Do

_____

_____

_____

_____

_____

What You Were Like

_____

_____

_____

_____

_____

Memorabilia

What Your Typical Day Was Like

_____

_____

_____

_____

_____

_____

Special People in Your Life

_____

_____

_____

_____

_____

Big Events

_____

_____

_____

_____

Memorabilia

Challenges

_____

_____

_____

_____

Stories and Other Tidbits

_____

_____

_____

_____

_____

_____

_____

_____

_____

_____

_____

_____

_____

_____

Memorabilia

YEAR 5 (4 YEARS OLD)

Your Favorite Things From This Year

Foods	
Toys	
Songs	
Shows	
Movies	
Activities	
Books	
Playmates	

Things We Did This Year

_____

_____

_____

_____

_____

_____

_____

_____

_____

_____

Memorabilia

Your Most Notable Developments and Achievements

_____

_____

_____

_____

_____

_____

Things You Loved to Do

_____

_____

_____

_____

_____

What You Were Like

_____

_____

_____

_____

_____

_____

Memorabilia

What Your Typical Day Was Like

_____

_____

_____

_____

_____

_____

Special People in Your Life

_____

_____

_____

_____

_____

Big Events

_____

_____

_____

_____

_____

Memorabilia

Challenges

_____

_____

_____

_____

Stories and Other Tidbits

_____

_____

_____

_____

_____

_____

_____

_____

_____

_____

_____

_____

_____

_____

_____

Memorabilia

YEAR 6 (5 YEARS OLD)

Your Favorite Things From This Year

Foods	
Toys	
Songs	
Shows	
Movies	
Activities	
Books	
Friends	

Things We Did This Year

_____

_____

_____

_____

_____

_____

_____

_____

_____

_____

_____

Memorabilia

Your Most Notable Achievements

_____

_____

_____

_____

_____

_____

Things You Loved to Do

_____

_____

_____

_____

_____

What You Were Like

_____

_____

_____

_____

_____

_____

Memorabilia

What Your Typical Day Was Like

_____

_____

_____

_____

_____

_____

Special People in Your Life

_____

_____

_____

_____

_____

Big Events

_____

_____

_____

_____

_____

Memorabilia

Challenges

_____

_____

_____

_____

Stories and Other Tidbits

_____

_____

_____

_____

_____

_____

_____

_____

_____

_____

_____

_____

_____

_____

_____

Memorabilia

YEAR 7 (6 YEARS OLD)

Your Favorite Things From This Year

Foods	Pancakes, Pizza, cereal, icecream
Toys	Barbie, LOL, magic box, Jenga, top trumps.
Songs	I'm a Barbie girl, The heart song (head + heart).
Shows	charlie + Choc, Jack + beanstalk, Matilda
Movies	Harry Potter, Ninja kids, Home Alone
Activities	Rainbows, Soft play, Swimming, gymnastics.
Books	The fox, mole horse. Little mermaid
Friends	Pollyanna, Grace, Millie + Eloise
	Daddy and Mummy.

Things We Did This Year

Snowball fight, Pillow fights, baking fighting (play fighting with Daddy).

Lion King, Charlie + chocolate factory + Matilda

Sunday pancakes.
Biking with Daddy

motorhome to scotland (June 2023).
Girls trip to London. (oct 2023)

Memorabilia

Your Most Notable Developments and Achievements

First 16 ~~mIke~~ mile bike ride
First time on TV and in a newspaper

Things You Loved to Do

Absolutely love Barbie, play with Barbie
doll house. Roller skating. Dancing, Rainbows
Swimming, gymnastics, tennis,

What You Were Like

Funny, creative, Kind, smiley,
Sharp/~~with~~ witty. Never gives up, Keeps
trying.

Memorabilia

What Your Typical Day Was Like

_____

_____

_____

_____

_____

_____

_____

Special People in Your Life

_____

_____

_____

_____

_____

_____

Big Events

_____

_____

_____

_____

_____

Memorabilia

Challenges

_____

_____

_____

_____

Stories and Other Tidbits

_____

_____

_____

_____

_____

_____

_____

_____

_____

_____

_____

_____

_____

_____

Memorabilia

Year 8 (7 Years Old)

Your Favorite Things From This Year

Foods	
Songs	
Shows	
Movies	
Activities	
Books	
Friends	

Things We Did This Year

_____

_____

_____

_____

_____

_____

_____

_____

_____

_____

Memorabilia

Your Most Notable Achievements

_____

_____

_____

_____

_____

_____

Things You Loved to Do

_____

_____

_____

_____

_____

_____

What You Were Like

_____

_____

_____

_____

_____

_____

Memorabilia

What Your Typical Day Was Like

_____

_____

_____

_____

_____

_____

Special People in Your Life

_____

_____

_____

_____

_____

Big Events

_____

_____

_____

_____

Memorabilia

Challenges

_____

_____

_____

_____

Stories and Other Tidbits

_____

_____

_____

_____

_____

_____

_____

_____

_____

_____

_____

_____

_____

_____

Memorabilia

YEAR 9 (8 YEARS OLD)

Your Favorite Things From This Year

Foods	
Songs	
Shows	
Movies	
Activities	
Books	
Friends	

Things We Did This Year

_____
_____
_____
_____
_____
_____
_____
_____
_____
_____
_____

Memorabilia

Your Most Notable Achievements

_____

_____

_____

_____

_____

_____

Things You Loved to Do

_____

_____

_____

_____

_____

What You Were Like

_____

_____

_____

_____

_____

Memorabilia

What Your Typical Day Was Like

_____

_____

_____

_____

_____

_____

Special People in Your Life

_____

_____

_____

_____

_____

_____

Big Events

_____

_____

_____

_____

_____

Memorabilia

Challenges

_____

_____

_____

_____

Stories and Other Tidbits

_____

_____

_____

_____

_____

_____

_____

_____

_____

_____

_____

_____

_____

Memorabilia

YEAR 10 (9 YEARS OLD)

Your Favorite Things From This Year

Foods	
Songs	
Shows	
Movies	
Activities	
Books	
Friends	

Things We Did This Year

_____

_____

_____

_____

_____

_____

_____

_____

_____

_____

_____

Memorabilia

Your Most Notable Achievements

_____

_____

_____

_____

_____

_____

Things You Loved to Do

_____

_____

_____

_____

_____

What You Were Like

_____

_____

_____

_____

_____

Memorabilia

What Your Typical Day Was Like

_____

_____

_____

_____

_____

_____

Special People in Your Life

_____

_____

_____

_____

_____

_____

Big Events

_____

_____

_____

_____

_____

Memorabilia

Challenges

_____

_____

_____

_____

Stories and Other Tidbits

_____

_____

_____

_____

_____

_____

_____

_____

_____

_____

_____

_____

_____

Memorabilia

Year 11 (10 Years Old)

Your Favorite Things From This Year

Foods	
Songs	
Shows	
Movies	
Activities	
Books	
Friends	

Things We Did This Year

_____

_____

_____

_____

_____

_____

_____

_____

_____

_____

_____

Memorabilia

Your Most Notable Achievements and Acts

_____

_____

_____

_____

_____

_____

Things You Loved to Do

_____

_____

_____

_____

_____

_____

What You Were Like

_____

_____

_____

_____

_____

Memorabilia

What Your Typical Day Was Like

_____

_____

_____

_____

_____

_____

Special People in Your Life

_____

_____

_____

_____

_____

Big Events

_____

_____

_____

_____

_____

Memorabilia

Challenges

_____

_____

_____

_____

Stories and Other Tidbits

_____

_____

_____

_____

_____

_____

_____

_____

_____

_____

_____

_____

_____

Memorabilia

Year 12 (11 Years Old)

Your Favorite Things From This Year

Foods	
Songs	
Shows	
Movies	
Activities	
Books	
Friends	

Things We Did This Year

_____

_____

_____

_____

_____

_____

_____

_____

_____

_____

_____

Memorabilia

Your Most Notable Achievements and Acts

_____

_____

_____

_____

_____

_____

Things You Loved to Do

_____

_____

_____

_____

_____

What You Were Like

_____

_____

_____

_____

_____

Memorabilia

What Your Typical Day Was Like

_____

_____

_____

_____

_____

_____

Special People in Your Life

_____

_____

_____

_____

_____

Big Events

_____

_____

_____

_____

_____

Memorabilia

Challenges

_____

_____

_____

_____

Stories and Other Tidbits

_____

_____

_____

_____

_____

_____

_____

_____

_____

_____

_____

_____

_____

Memorabilia

Year 13 (12 Years Old)

Your Favorite Things From This Year

Foods	
Songs	
Shows	
Movies	
Activities	
Books	
Friends	

Things We Did This Year

_____

_____

_____

_____

_____

_____

_____

_____

_____

_____

Memorabilia

Your Most Notable Achievements and Acts

_____

_____

_____

_____

_____

_____

Things You Loved to Do

_____

_____

_____

_____

_____

What You Were Like

_____

_____

_____

_____

_____

_____

Memorabilia

What Your Typical Day Was Like

_____

_____

_____

_____

_____

_____

Special People in Your Life

_____

_____

_____

_____

_____

Big Events

_____

_____

_____

_____

_____

Memorabilia

Challenges

_____

_____

_____

_____

Stories and Other Tidbits

_____

_____

_____

_____

_____

_____

_____

_____

_____

_____

_____

_____

_____

_____

Memorabilia

YEAR 14 (13 YEARS OLD)

Your Favorite Things From This Year

Foods	
Songs	
Shows	
Movies	
Activities	
Books	
Friends	

Things We Did This Year

_____

_____

_____

_____

_____

_____

_____

_____

_____

_____

_____

Memorabilia

Your Most Notable Achievements and Acts

_____

_____

_____

_____

_____

_____

Things You Loved to Do

_____

_____

_____

_____

_____

_____

What You Were Like

_____

_____

_____

_____

_____

_____

Memorabilia

What Your Typical Day Was Like

_____

_____

_____

_____

_____

_____

Special People in Your Life

_____

_____

_____

_____

_____

Big Events

_____

_____

_____

_____

_____

Memorabilia

Challenges

_____

_____

_____

_____

Stories and Other Tidbits

_____

_____

_____

_____

_____

_____

_____

_____

_____

_____

_____

_____

_____

Memorabilia

YEAR 15 (14 YEARS OLD)

Your Favorite Things From This Year

Foods	
Songs	
Shows	
Movies	
Activities	
Books	
Friends	

Things We Did This Year

_____

_____

_____

_____

_____

_____

_____

_____

_____

_____

Memorabilia

Your Most Notable Achievements and Acts

_____

_____

_____

_____

_____

_____

Things You Loved to Do

_____

_____

_____

_____

_____

What You Were Like

_____

_____

_____

_____

_____

Memorabilia

What Your Typical Day Was Like

_____

_____

_____

_____

_____

_____

Special People in Your Life

_____

_____

_____

_____

_____

Big Events

_____

_____

_____

_____

_____

Memorabilia

Challenges

_____

_____

_____

_____

Stories and Other Tidbits

_____

_____

_____

_____

_____

_____

_____

_____

_____

_____

_____

_____

_____

Memorabilia

YEAR 16 (15 YEARS OLD)

Your Favorite Things From This Year

Foods	
Songs	
Shows	
Movies	
Activities	
Books	
Friends	

Things We Did This Year

_____

_____

_____

_____

_____

_____

_____

_____

_____

_____

_____

Memorabilia

Your Most Notable Achievements and Acts

_____

_____

_____

_____

_____

_____

Things You Loved to Do

_____

_____

_____

_____

_____

What You Were Like

_____

_____

_____

_____

_____

Memorabilia

What Your Typical Day Was Like

_____

_____

_____

_____

_____

_____

Special People in Your Life

_____

_____

_____

_____

_____

Big Events

_____

_____

_____

_____

_____

Memorabilia

Challenges

_____

_____

_____

_____

Stories and Other Tidbits

_____

_____

_____

_____

_____

_____

_____

_____

_____

_____

_____

_____

_____

Memorabilia

Year 17 (16 Years Old)

Your Favorite Things From This Year

Foods	
Songs	
Shows	
Movies	
Activities	
Books	
Friends	

Things We Did This Year

_____

_____

_____

_____

_____

_____

_____

_____

_____

_____

_____

Memorabilia

Your Most Notable Developments

_____

_____

_____

_____

_____

Things You Loved to Do

_____

_____

_____

_____

_____

What You Were Like

_____

_____

_____

_____

_____

Memorabilia

What Your Typical Day Was Like

_____

_____

_____

_____

_____

_____

Special People in Your Life

_____

_____

_____

_____

_____

_____

Big Events

_____

_____

_____

_____

_____

Memorabilia

Challenges

_____

_____

_____

_____

Stories and Other Tidbits

_____

_____

_____

_____

_____

_____

_____

_____

_____

_____

_____

_____

Memorabilia

YEAR 18 (17 YEARS OLD)

Your Favorite Things From This Year

Foods	
Songs	
Shows	
Movies	
Activities	
Books	
Friends	

Things We Did This Year

_____

_____

_____

_____

_____

_____

_____

_____

_____

_____

_____

Memorabilia

Your Most Notable Achievements and Acts

_____

_____

_____

_____

_____

_____

Things You Loved to Do

_____

_____

_____

_____

_____

What You Were Like

_____

_____

_____

_____

_____

Memorabilia

What Your Typical Day Was Like

_____

_____

_____

_____

_____

_____

Special People in Your Life

_____

_____

_____

_____

_____

_____

Big Events

_____

_____

_____

_____

_____

Memorabilia

Challenges

_____

_____

_____

_____

Stories and Other Tidbits

_____

_____

_____

_____

_____

_____

_____

_____

_____

_____

_____

_____

_____

_____

Memorabilia

May the rest of your years be as fulfilling as the first 18.
Remember that you are always loved.

Printed in Great Britain
by Amazon

30096134R00086